BEYOND THE THEORY: SCIENCE OF THE FUTURE

IS TIME TRAVEL POSSIBLE?

THEORIES ABOUT TIME

Tom Jackson

Gareth Stevens
PUBLISHING

Please visit our website, www.garethstevens.com.
For a free color catalog of all our high-quality books,
call toll free 1-800-542-2595 or fax 1-877-542-2596.

Cataloging-in-Publication Data

Names: Jackson, Tom.
Title: Is time travel possible? theories about time / Tom Jackson.
Description: New York : Gareth Stevens Publishing, 2019. | Series: Beyond the theory: science of the future |
Includes glossary and index.
Identifiers: LCCN ISBN 9781538226629 (pbk.) | ISBN 9781538226612 (library bound)
Subjects: LCSH: Space and time--Juvenile literature. | Time travel--Juvenile literature. |
Time--Juvenile literature.
Classification: LCC QC173.59.S65 J33 2019 | DDC 530.11--dc23

First Edition

Published in 2019 by
Gareth Stevens Publishing
111 East 14th Street, Suite 349
New York, NY 10003

© 2019 Gareth Stevens Publishing

Produced for Gareth Stevens by Calcium
Editors: Sarah Eason and Tim Cooke
Designers: Emma DeBanks and Lynne Lennon
Picture researcher: Rachel Blount

Picture credits: Cover: Shutterstock: Hayati Kayhan: foreground, Nazar Yosyfiv: background; Inside:
Shutterstock: Algol: p. 5; Kryvenok Anastasiia: p. 11; Giacomo Baudazzi: p. 34; Cybrain: p. 25; DeltaOFF:
p. 4; Everett Historical: p. 28; Juergen Faelchle: p. 40; General-fmv: p. 37; GiroScience: p. 24; Images By Kenny:
p. 16; David Ionut: p. 22; Sergey Kamshylin: p. 6; Hayati Kayhan: p. 7; Kerenby: p. 43; Fred Mantel: pp. 1, 42;
Martinova4: p. 33; Marzolino: p. 17; Metha1819: p. 13; MichaelTaylor: p. 9r; Monkey Business Images: p. 31;
NeonSho: p. 29; Peshkova: p. 30; Photobank Gallery: p. 20; PhotographyByMK: p. 23; Posteriori: p. 27; Paul
Prescott: p. 32; White Pudica: p. 21; Serg64: p. 12; Still Life Photography: p. 18; Studiovin: p. 10; Marina Sun:
p. 41; Triff: p. 14; Vexworldwide: pp. 8-9; Wikimedia Commons: p. 15; Maahmaah: p. 19; NASA, ESA, J. Hester
and A. Loll (Arizona State University): p. 39; NASA; ESA; G. Illingworth, D. Magee, and P. Oesch, University
of California, Santa Cruz; R. Bouwens, Leiden University; and the HUDF09 Team: p. 36; Mike Peel
(www.mikepeel.net): p. 35; Ferdinand Schmutzer: p. 26; Skatebiker: p. 38.

Printed in the United States of America

CPSIA compliance information: Batch #CS18GS:
For further information contact Gareth Stevens, New York, New York at 1-800-542-2595.

CONTENTS

CHAPTER 1

THINKING
TIME

What time is it? That is a common question with an easy answer. However, it is also one of the strangest things we can ask. There is almost no other question where the answer is always changing and never the same twice.

Life without time is unthinkable. There would be no birthdays. No one would get old—and no one would be born. For scientists, time is one of the fundamental **dimensions** that help us make sense of the universe. But the more we think about time, the weirder it appears. When we talk about time, are we measuring and monitoring a real thing, or is time just a useful idea we have invented?

Ruins from the past help us imagine living in those times.

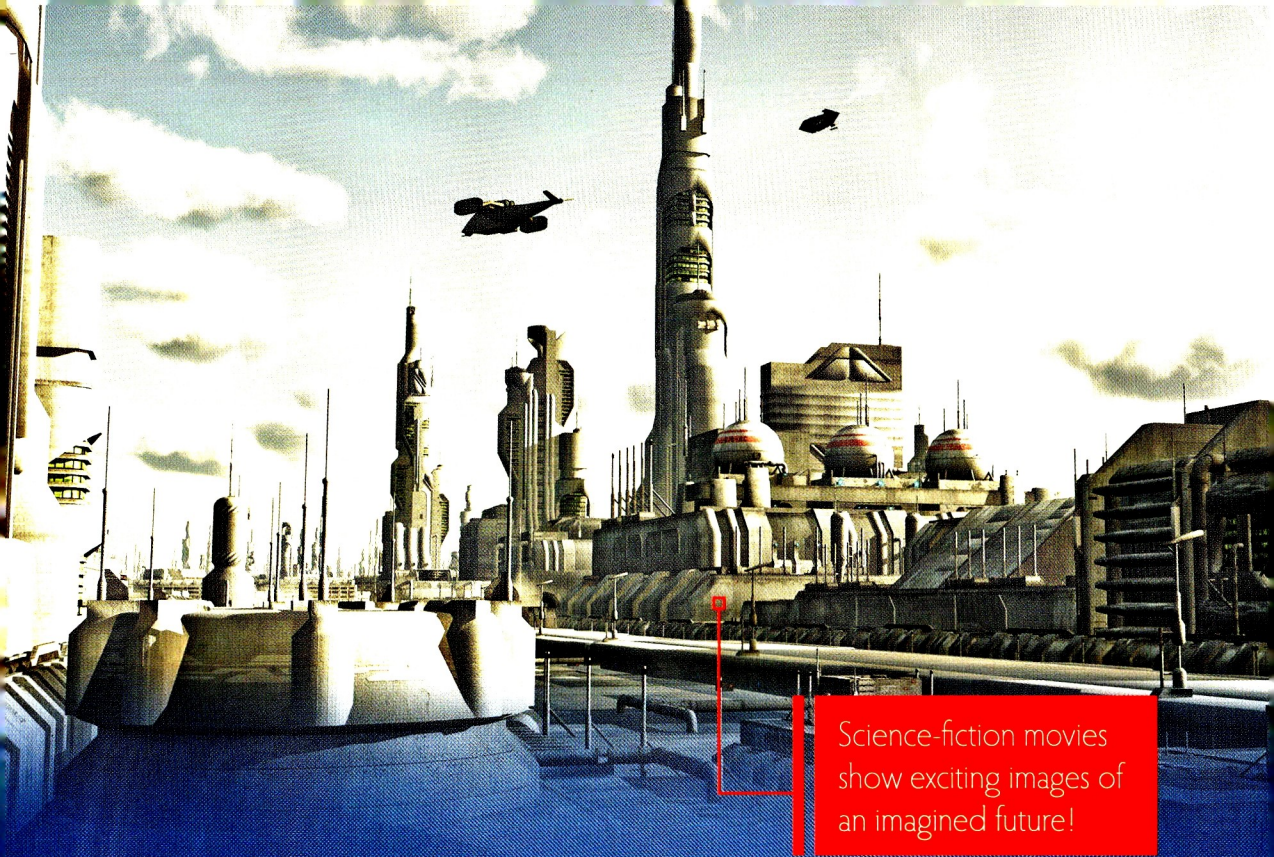

For centuries, people have been attracted to the idea of being able to travel in time. Artists and writers have imagined life in the past. Who would not want to visit a lost ancient civilization or witness great moments in history for themselves? No one is sure whether that may ever be possible. Whatever technology scientists invent, the laws of **physics** seem to be stacked against going back into the past—and those laws can never be broken (which is itself one of the laws of physics).

How about traveling to the future? What will life be like in the year 3000? There is already one easy way to find out: just stay alive for the next 980 years or so. All of us are time travelers to the future. In fact, it is impossible for us to do anything other than travel into the future, because time as we perceive it can never be stopped.

Could we speed up time, so we wouldn't have to wait over 900 years to get to the year 3000? According to the laws of physics, this is possible … in theory. Even now—whenever "now" is—some of us are moving through time very slightly faster than others. A technology that would make travel into the future **practical** is beyond our current capabilities—but it might eventually become possible one day. To find out what the future holds, we will have to go beyond the theory.

WHAT IS TIME?

Right now you are reading this word: ding. Reading "ding" was an event in time. But what came first, the time or the event? Is time a series of events, or are events just evidence of the passing of time? That is a very tricky question to understand, let alone answer. We can look at it in other ways.

There are two main ways of picturing time. In the first one, time is already filled with events from the past, present, and future. Future events will always turn into present events, which then become past events.

A bell ringing "ding dong" might seem simple, but it raises many questions about the nature of time.

In this understanding of time, you read "ding" in the past. At that time, your reading of "dong"—now—was a future event, which then became the present as you read it and is now in the past. So both events are locations in time that already existed in a vast, unchanging collection of events.

The second way of looking at time turns the first one on its head. In this version, time is simply humans' way of ordering events. In other words, it explains that you read "ding" before "dong," not the other way around. There was also a clear period of time between those two events. The difference is that the events make the time, and events only exist in the present. They are caused by events that are now in the past and will themselves cause new events in the future—but neither the future nor the past actually exist.

UNANSWERED

There is a third possible view of time, which is a halfway position between the two main views. It says that future events are uncertain and not yet real. They are caused by events that take place in the present and then become the past: You read "ding" and were so fascinated that you continued until you got to "dong," and now you are here. Hello! Those past events are now real; they happened and will exist in the past forever.

A FOURTH DIMENSION

Scientists measure things based on seven fundamental features, or base units. The first five are **mass**, temperature, brightness, quantity, and electric charge. These are all properties of **matter**. The final two units measure distance and time—where the matter is and *when* it is. Distance and time are used to measure things such as speed, acceleration, and forces such as **gravity**.

We see the world in three spatial dimensions. Objects have height, length, and width, and their location in space changes our perspective of them. That's why big things look small when they are far away.

Even with only three spatial dimensions, artists can construct baffling versions of reality.

UNANSWERED

We perceive the world in three dimensions of space and one of time—but that does not mean the universe is structured with four dimensions. String theory is a way of understanding energy and matter as tiny vibrations at the smallest, **quantum** scale of space. Physicists say that the theory only works if there are 11 dimensions: the four we know about and seven other compact dimensions that can only be seen when they look deep inside subatomic **particles**.

In string theory, energy and matter exist as tiny vibrations in space.

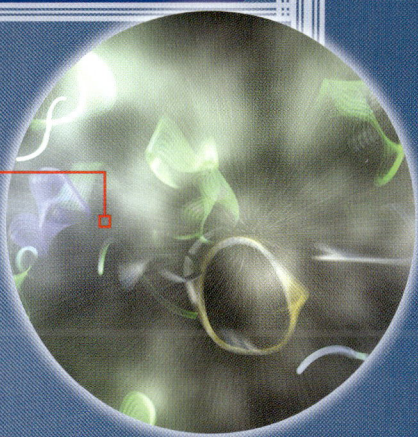

Time is often called the fourth dimension, but how is it linked to the three spatial dimensions? A dot has zero dimensions; it is a point in space. A line has two dimensions, a length but no width or height. A second line branching off the first has moved into the second dimension. Lines using two dimensions can make flat shapes that have length and width. Lines rising from the flat shape are moving into the third dimension, giving a height measurement. Now for the fourth dimension. No object exists forever, so its spatial dimensions will change at some point, perhaps due to physical events such as collisions or chemical reactions. We measure the way the object changes as time. Therefore, as well as having a length and position in space, every object has a length and position in time.

ORDER
AND CHAOS

The four dimensions of space and time describe what is going on, but do not explain why change happens. If the three spatial dimensions never changed, and the objects they describe never changed location, there would be no need for a fourth dimension. Time would stand still—but that is something time does not do.

Clothes thrown onto the floor never fold themselves into a tidy pile. Try it for yourself!

According to physics, time is caused by a quality called **entropy**. Entropy is a way of understanding how energy behaves, a field of science called thermodynamics. Physicists have four laws of thermodynamics. The second law says that an object—or more likely a whole system of objects—will always gain entropy.

Entropy is sometimes described as a measure of disorder. It is the reason why dumping out the contents of a neat sock drawer always makes a jumbled pile, and why a jumble of clothes will never pack itself neatly when dropped into a drawer. Another way to understand entropy is to see it as energy spreading out. A fresh cup of coffee has low entropy because its energy is concentrated inside it in the form of heat. That energy moves randomly but ends up spreading out. As a result, the coffee cools as its energy is transferred to the surroundings.

BEHIND THE THEORY

The idea of entropy came from Rudolf Clausius, a nineteenth-century German physicist. He used it to describe how energy was being used by steam engines—and his ideas are true for any machine. Due to entropy, not all the energy fed into any engine can be used to create motion. Some of it is always lost as **friction**, heat, or some other useless form of energy. This is why machines need a constant supply of energy in order to function.

In theory, it is possible for energy to move the other way, so the coffee actually gets hotter and the surroundings get colder. In reality, however, this is so unlikely that it never happens.

As well as making hot things cool down and cold things warm up, entropy is the reason chemical reactions occur. It is also why all objects, from stars and stone monuments to a human body, will eventually break apart. It is only a matter of time.

Heat energy spreads out—so your coffee gets cold.

CHAPTER 2

PHILOSOPHY OF TIME

Science does not have all the answers when it comes to the nature of time. Philosophers have also tried to describe it. Philosophers have a different approach than that of scientists. They wonder about things that cannot be observed or measured that scientists ignore.

Philosophers who study time are divided into two main types depending on their ideas. They are either "presentists" or "eternalists." A presentist philosopher argues that the past and the future do not exist, so that all that does exist is the present. This is the same as the theory that time is the product of a sequence of events, each caused by the ones before and causing more events to follow.

A movie creates motion through a rapid sequence of still images, or moments.

Presentist philosophers are interested in how people perceive time as a series of instant "nows." Each now flashes from one to the next, like the frames of a movie. In every instant, the old present is destroyed and a new one forms, only to be destroyed by the next, and so on.

A presentist sees time as a point with no length that is moving from the future toward the past. For example, presentists argue that dinosaurs do not exist. They did exist in long-ago presents, but now they do not—although some of their bones and fossils do exist in the present.

An eternalist philosopher would say that dinosaurs exist just as much as you or me—but they exist in the past. They see time as a line, with the dinosaurs somewhere along the line in the distant past and us at the point marked as present. Eternalists also think the line extends into the future, so as well as dinosaurs and you, the timeline also contains amazing new innovations like a moon base or flying cars.

Neither of these philosophical views of time align with the scientific understanding of the universe—but does that make them incorrect? Which one are you, a presentist or an eternalist?

In some views of time, dinosaurs still exist. They are simply in the past.

DID TIME START?

The best theory scientists have about the start of the universe is known as the Big Bang. Astronomers have gathered a huge amount of evidence that shows that the universe started out very small and hot. It has expanded and cooled ever since, forming the vast space we see today.

The Big Bang occurred 13.8 billion years ago. In a moment, it created all of space and the energy within space. So did the Big Bang create all of time, too? Given that science understands time as a description of changes within space, driven by entropy and the spreading of energy, could time exist before space and energy? Scientists currently think the universe will end in the Big Rip. All matter and energy will be spread remarkably thinly across an expanding universe trillions of times bigger than now. This would be maximum entropy, so all physical change would stop. Everything would be cold and inactive, a state physicists call Heat Death.

The expansion of the universe began in a single moment that created all space and energy.

BEHIND THE THEORY

The thirteenth-century Italian monk Thomas Aquinas tried to solve a contradiction in Christian teaching. At the time, the Church taught that God had created the universe, which was perfect and unchanging, and would exist forever. Some scholars wondered how something could have a beginning and yet be **infinite** and never-ending. There must have been a time before the universe began. Aquinas's fix was to say that God did create the universe, but at the same time, he made it so it had always existed.

However, time would continue. A clock would keep counting the time, even if the universe had stopped doing anything. Now that time has started, it is hard to see how it could ever stop again. But can time ever start? Early thinkers such as the ancient Greek philosopher Aristotle and the Italian Renaissance astronomer Galileo Galilei said the universe started with a first movement that got everything going, including time. They said that first movement was provided by an Unmoved Mover. In their own ways, science and philosophy or religion are both trying to explain what or who the Unmoved Mover is.

Christians believe God started the universe.

LIKE
CLOCKWORK

In the early nineteenth century, the French scientist Pierre-Simon Laplace considered many problems, including how heat worked and how planets and stars all moved around in space. Laplace investigated these questions using laws of motion developed over a century earlier by the English scientist Isaac Newton.

Newton said the universe worked like clockwork. He showed how it functioned by coming up with famous ideas about gravity and motion. Newton did not mean the solar system was made up of cogs, like a watch. Instead, he meant that all objects were connected, so they worked as a whole. For example, he believed heat and light were particles in constant collision with one another, like balls on a pool table. A change in motion in one body affected the motion of all the others.

Newton imagined motion as a series of collisions between particles, like balls.

Newton's mathematics worked well for two moving objects but got complicated for three or more. Laplace imagined a demon that could solve all the complex sums, and therefore knew the speed and direction of all particles in the universe and where they would go next—forever. Laplace realized that, if math could predict the exact behavior of **atoms** and stars, the future of the universe must already be locked into its present arrangement. That meant that every thought, every movement, every idea he had was already **predetermined** by the fixed nature of the universe. In other words, he had no **free will**, or no control over his future.

Being able to predict the future—and traveling into it—could mean we have no choice about the direction of our lives. Does that sound like a good thing? Read on to find out more—perhaps you have no choice!

Pierre-Simon Laplace worried that a predictable future was a sign that humans lacked the ability to make their own choices.

UNANSWERED

Chaos theory is a type of mathematics that shows that even tiny changes in complex processes can make the end result very different. This is sometimes called the Butterfly Effect. Say a weather system is forming over the Sahara Desert. Add in the effect of the flutter of a single butterfly's wings, and the system might eventually be transformed into a catastrophic hurricane. Chaos theory shows that even if the future is created according to a set of rules, such as Newton's laws of motion, the future is still unpredictable.

17

CHAPTER 3

MEASURING TIME

Are you someone who is always on time or are you often late? And how do you know anyway? If no one is sure what time really is, or whether it is real, does it even matter?

Whatever the answer to the question, since ancient days, humans have had a sense of time passing. Over time, we have steadily developed methods of measuring it. There are two devices to do this. A clock marks the passage of time, while a timer measures how long a particular process takes.

A sundial uses an arm to cast a shadow as the sun moves in the sky.

The first clocks were sundials, which were invented in ancient Egypt about 3,500 years ago. Sundials cast the shadow of the sun onto a dial or wall. The moving shadow tracks the motion of the sun from sunrise to sunset. Sundials are still familiar today, but modern horology—the science of timekeeping—has moved on so much that there are far more accurate ways to measure time.

Timer technology is probably even older than sundials. The first timer might have been the clepsydra, or water clock. The earliest evidence for them comes from China about 6,000 years ago. The idea is simple. Someone fills a bowl with a set volume of water, which then drips out through a small hole at the base. Expert craftsmen ensured that each water clock had the same volume and the same size drip hole, so that each takes the same amount of time to empty out.

Water clocks and sand timers, which used a similar technique, were used to measure specific amounts of time throughout the day. In ancient Greek the word for "a period of time" was *hora*, which gives us the modern word *hour*. In ancient civilizations, people had no need to measure time more accurately than by the hour. Today we can measure time a lot more accurately. The most accurate modern clocks measure time not in hours or minutes but in 100-trillionths of a second.

NATURAL CYCLES

The measurement of time is based on natural events that occur at different rates. The most obvious is the day–night cycle, which is the apparent motion of the sun through the sky, rising at dawn and setting at dusk. The sun only appears to move. What is really happening is that Earth is spinning and each rotation takes a fixed time, which we call a day.

The cycle of seasons—from winter to spring, summer, and fall—takes longer. The seasons occur due to changing conditions caused by the motion of Earth around the sun. A full cycle fits into the time it takes for the planet to make one **orbit**. This is another fixed amount of time, which we call the year.

There are roughly 365 days in a year. Those days are divided into weeks and months, time periods based on the behavior of the moon. Every 28 days, the moon goes through phases. It begins as a full moon, then becomes a waning or shrinking half moon. It then becomes a new moon, when it is barely visible.

Earth's motion around the sun creates the changes that define the four seasons.

The main part of Stonehenge was a circle of standing stones.

UNANSWERED

Stonehenge in southern England is one of the world's most famous ancient monuments. It was built by farming peoples between about 3100 and 1600 BC. No one is sure what it was built for, but the monument appears to be aligned with the motion of the sun through the year. The best guess is that Stonehenge was partly a temple and partly an astronomical **observatory**, where priests watched out for the most important days of each year.

It then becomes a waxing, or growing, half moon, before finally becoming a full moon again. Each of these four phases takes seven days to complete, a period of time we now call a week.

The Babylonians of ancient Iraq thought there were just 360 days in the year, so they divided it into 12 months of 30 days. It would have been more accurate to have 13 months of 28 days, but the Babylonians always counted things in 60s or numbers that divided into 60. The mistake was never corrected, just tweaked into the somewhat irregular modern calendar.

We have the Egyptians to thank for the 12-hour day (and night). Their sundials were divided into 10 sectors. The hours after dawn and before dusk, when the sundial did not cast a shadow, were added as two more hours. The minute comes from the Latin word for "small part," and minutes were further divided into "second small parts," or seconds. Again, the math of ancient Babylon is why we still count minutes and seconds in 60s.

TIMEKEEPING

Just as people's basic sense of time passing is based on the rhythms of nature, technology uses other rhythms, called **oscillations**, to measure time. Clocks have used different oscillators, from swinging weights and bouncing springs to vibrating crystals and energized atoms.

In the Midde Ages, time was most important for religious people such as monks and nuns, who needed to know when to pray. By the thirteenth century, many churches and monasteries had primitive mechanical clocks. They lowered a weight down from a great height in a fixed amount of time. Such clocks were often highly inaccurate, however, and the weight needed to be "wound up" several times a day.

This clock was built to measure astronomical movements in Prague in 1410.

The first accurate clocks used swinging arms called pendulums. Pendulum clocks were based on the pendulum law discovered in the seventeenth century by Galileo Galilei. He realized that a pendulum always takes the same amount of time to swing, no matter how hard it is pushed. The period, or time of each swing, is governed by the pendulum's length. Soon, clocks were using pendulums. A 39-inch (99 cm) pendulum swings with a period of one second, so such clocks are often tall.

BEHIND THE THEORY

The story goes that scientist Galileo Galilei discovered the pendulum law while attending mass inside Pisa Cathedral in Italy. A large candle lamp was suspended from the ceiling. As a church official lit the lamp, he set it swinging, and Galileo noticed that it always swung with the same period. He used his own pulse as a timer to confirm his theory.

Springs oscillate with the same type of motion as a pendulum, but are much smaller. By the eighteenth century, spring-powered watches could fit in a pocket. Today's watches—and most clocks—use **quartz** oscillators. When electrified, these crystals vibrate at 32,768 times a second.

Even that is not good enough for the most accurate clocks. Official time is kept with **atomic clocks** with quartz oscillators. The vibrations are kept accurate using the behavior of **heavy metals**, most often caesium, which absorb and release energy regularly. Caesium controls the electrical supply to the quartz and keeps it wobbling in a near-perfect rhythm. The best atomic clocks lose only one second every 300 million years!

A clock's pendulum swings at a fixed rate.

23

CHAPTER 4

MOVING IN TIME

According to the presentist school of thought, time travel does not make any sense. The presentist theory is that only the present exists. In this view, the universe is a series of **instantaneous** states that constantly change from one to the next. Traveling to the future or the past is not possible because there is simply nothing to travel to.

Eternalist philosophy is more in keeping with scientific evidence—although not completely. This view says that time is a line. The points along that line are different places in history, which we call the present, the past, and the future. Time travelers could visit other times by changing their position on the line, in the same way they can change their positions in space.

Does time connect our world to a series of similar worlds in the past and present?

In a way, we are already doing that. Our position on the line of time is always moving, shifting toward the future and away from the past. So we are already time travelers. In theory, that means we should be able to travel into the future simply by moving quicker through time. However, that would require us to change our understanding of the rules of physics. Slowing down in time, in contrast, would not make us go into the past. We would just reach the future at a slower pace. To go back to the past, we would need to reverse the flow of time itself—and that is something that is not possible.

Although traveling to the future may be possible in theory, traveling to the past is simply not possible.

A final problem is that humans cannot experience anything beyond a single line, or dimension, of time. Perhaps the line of time can branch in different directions, making it a "timeshape" rather than a timeline. In that case, what past or future would we be traveling into? Would it be our own or an alternative? We simply do not know because no one has ever traveled in time—not on our current timeline of history, anyway.

MOTION IN
SPACE AND TIME

In the early twentieth century, Albert Einstein, a young German office worker, had one of the most brilliant thoughts in history. That thought became the theory of relativity—and changed our view of time forever.

Einstein was thinking about a big problem in physics. Newton's laws of motion described how two cars driving toward each other were traveling at a faster relative speed—measured by comparing their speeds—than two cars driving in the same direction. However, in the nineteenth century, Scottish scientist James Clark Maxwell said that light always traveled at the same speed. How could both things be true? The beams from the car headlights, moving in either direction, all moved along at the same speed. According to Newton's laws, light from an approaching car is moving faster, because the car is also moving toward you at the same time. But all measurements say otherwise. The speed of light is always constant, no matter how fast its source is moving.

Albert Einstein, photographed in 1921.

BEHIND THE THEORY

Einstein began thinking about relativity when he was a teenager. He wondered what he would see if he could sit on a light beam, traveling at the speed of light. If Newton's system of motion was correct, light coming from the front would reach his eyes, but if he turned around, light from behind would never be able to go faster than him and catch up. So half of his view would be completely black. This did not make sense to the young man—and his solution to the problem made him the greatest scientist in history.

Einstein came up with a mind-bending solution to the problem. As an object with mass, such as a car, moves faster and faster through space, it moves slower and slower through time. The full idea is far more complex, involving the theory that energy alters the shape of space, **warping** it into ripples. The effects all work together so that measuring the speed of light always produces the same result, no matter how fast it is moving.

Nevertheless, Einstein's ideas about relativity showed a way to travel in time. Perhaps you are time traveling right now? Turn the page to find out.

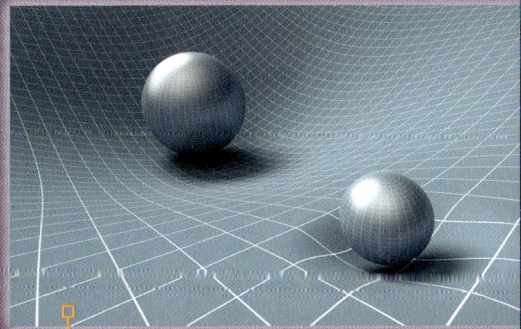

According to the theory of relativity, objects warp both space and time.

TWIN
PARADOX

The theory of relativity is hard to understand because it does not match how we experience the world. At low speeds—even flying in a plane—the effects of relativity are so tiny that we never notice them. However, scientists have used super-accurate atomic clocks to measure the effects of relativity.

Space travel has proved Einstein's theories right.

One clock stays at the airport. Another is placed on a fast jet aircraft and taken for a high-speed flight. When the plane lands, the clocks no longer show the same time. The one on the plane is now a fraction of second behind the other because it traveled slower through time during its flight.

This experiment proves one of Einstein's most famous thought experiments. Einstein imagined a pair of twins, one of whom was a space adventurer. This twin boarded a rocket and blasted off into space, traveling about half the speed of light—13,500 times faster than today's space rockets. The twin spends a year living in space. When he returns to Earth, his earthbound twin is an old man.

BEHIND THE THEORY

The National Aeronautics and Space Administration (NASA) tested Einstein's twin **paradox**. In 2016, Scott Kelly returned after spending almost a year in space on the International Space Station. His twin, Mark, had stayed on Earth. Scott was six minutes older than Mark when he launched—but six minutes and five milliseconds older when he landed! NASA was more interested in how Scott's body had been changed by life in space, comparing it to that of his earthbound identical twin.

Time on Earth has proceeded more quickly, and the twins have aged at different rates. By traveling very fast through space, the space twin has effectively traveled into the future. The same slowing of time occurs when space is warped. Heavy objects, such as stars or black holes, bend the space around them, making time slow down. The space twin could travel even further into the future by flying through space warped by a black hole. Earth warps space, too, so time moves slower the closer you are to the center of the planet. That means people who live in a basement are younger (by a very tiny amount) than their neighbors upstairs.

Twins would age at different speeds if one were in space.

ARROW
OF TIME

It's already possible to go to the future. All you need to do is speed up time by warping space, by either using a large mass of energy or by traveling at a very high speed. Simple!

However, a time traveler would have to be brave. At best, they would arrive in a future where technology has advanced, in which case the time traveler would be like a prehistoric human appearing today. In the worst case, the traveler might find that society has collapsed— or even that humans have destroyed the world. Oh well, they could just come back to the present. But wait—could they?

We often imagine the future as a better world—but it might also be far worse than the present!

Time is often likened to an arrow. It has a clear direction. We all move forward with the arrow of time, but there is no mechanism to make it go backward. The direction of time has to be fixed. That is how scientists make their theories of space and time work

According to relativity, an object that could move backward in time would need a negative mass—it has to weigh less than nothing. Such an object would slow down when you gave it more energy (normal objects speed up), and it could travel faster than light. It would be impossible to ever see it coming, but it would leave a shockwave as it broke the "light barrier." Such a strange object is termed a tachyon. Physicists do look for them, but no one actually expects to find one.

Time can only move in one direction partly because of one of the most important features of the universe: **causality**. According to causality, every event has a cause and effect. A cause in the past created an event, and the effect of that present event will create the next event in the future. If it were possible to go backward in time, that would break causality. The cause and effect of the time traveler would be traveling in the reverse direction, with causes coming from the future and affecting the past.

This is summed up as the Grandfather Paradox. A time traveler goes back in time and kills his own grandfather, before the birth of his father. That means his father is never born, nor is the time traveler, so there is no one to go back in time in the first place. Everything we know about the links between light, energy, space, and time tells us that traveling to the past is simply impossible.

If a time traveler kills his own grandfather, how can he ever be born?

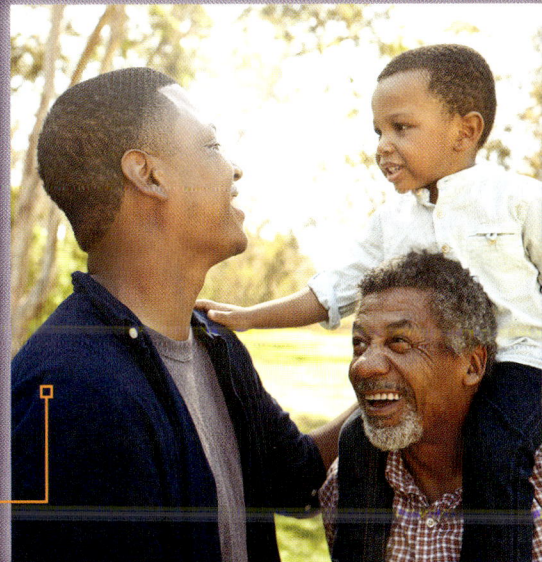

CHAPTER 5

CONTROLLING TIME

Time is vital to everyday life. We need it to catch a train, get to school on time, and cook our food until it is good to eat. Clocks tells us when it is time to work and when to take a break. Without time, we would not know when to go on vacation, when our birthday is, or even how old we are.

That is why the science of time is so confusing. Time is not meant to speed up and slow down. It is supposed to stay constant—and go like clockwork. Luckily, we can ignore the strange effects of relativity in everyday life. Instead, we impose a well-organized and very precise system called UTC, or Universal Coordinated Time, which means that, wherever you are, you can always be sure of the time. And UTC offers us our only realistic chance of being time travelers.

Without using time, it would be impossible to travel to school or work.

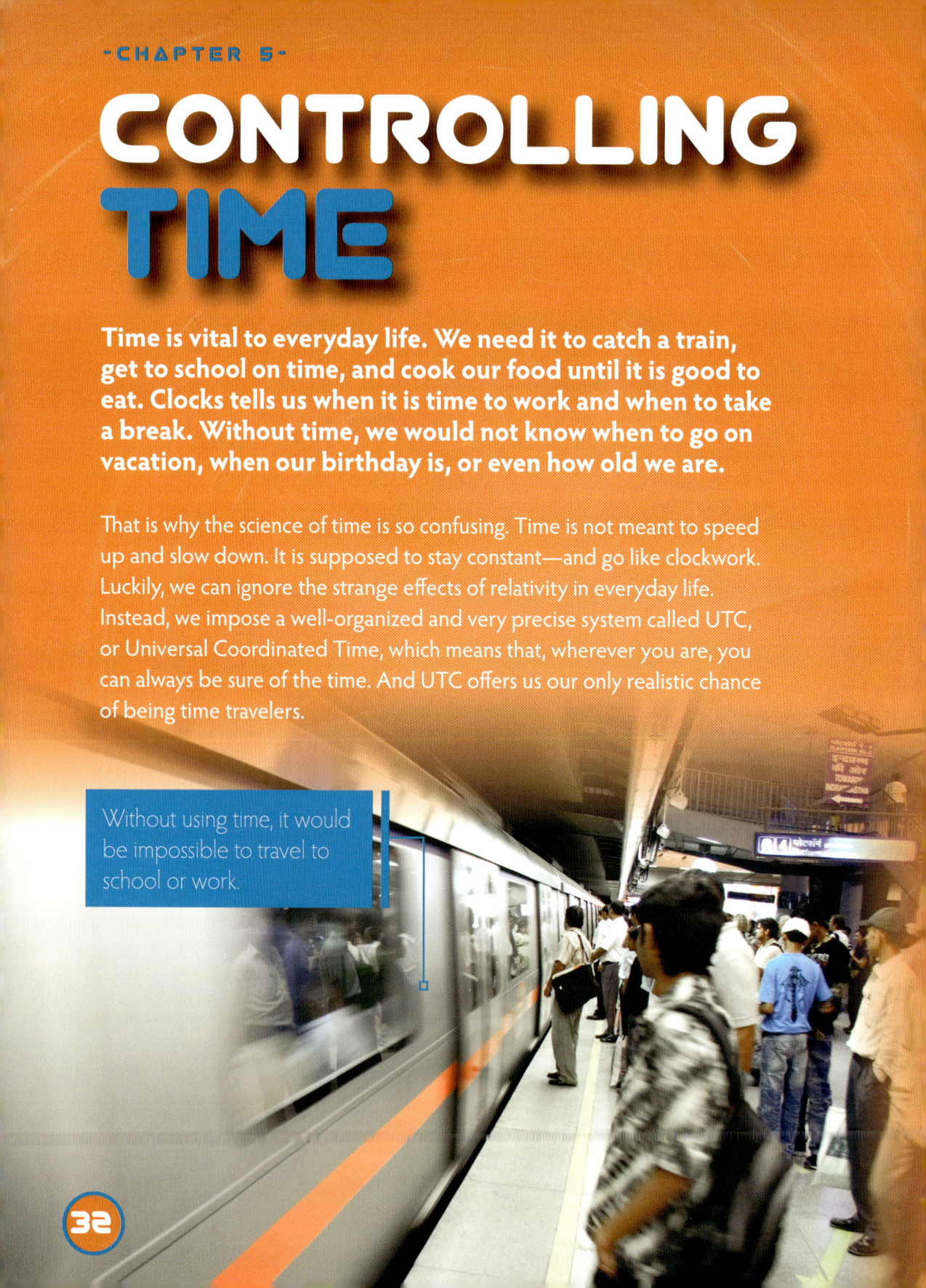

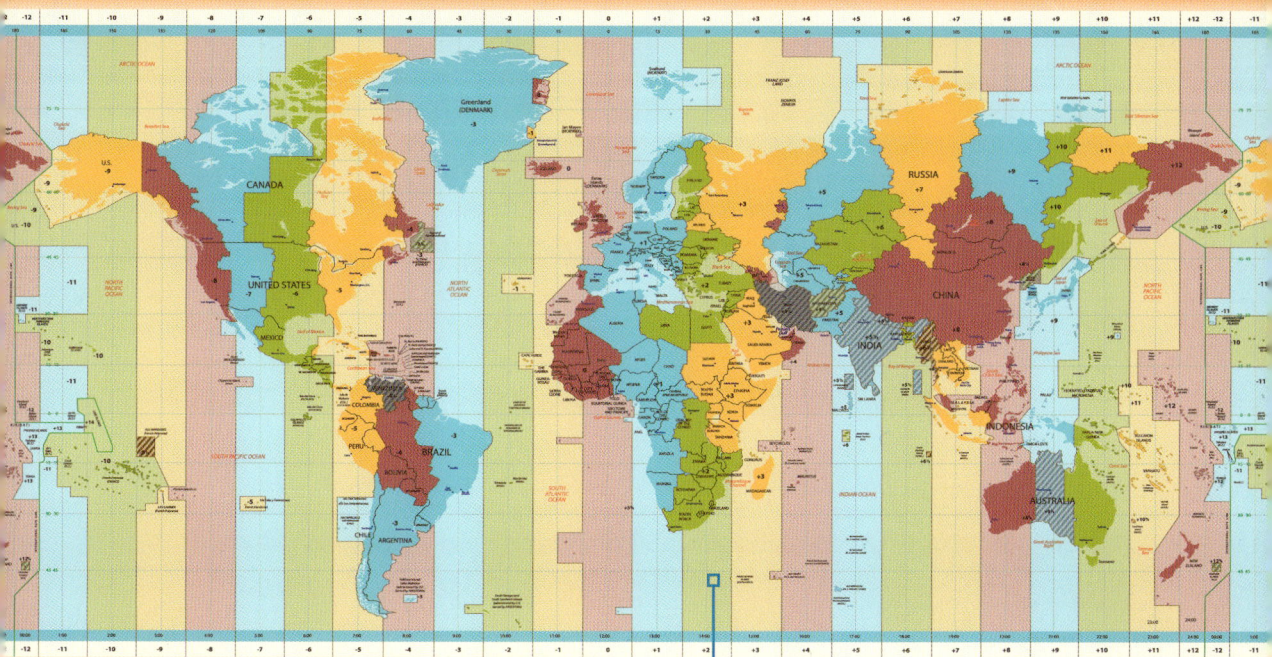

The 24 time zones have irregular edges because they fit the borders of countries and regions.

The idea of UTC was adopted in the 1880s. Before that, the best way to tell the time was to look at the sun. When it was at its highest point in the sky, directly overhead, the time had to be midday, or 12:00 p.m. However, midday—like the timings of sunrise and sunset—varies from place to place as Earth turns and the sun appears to move from east to west through the sky.

UTC divides the world into time zones, which are strips running from pole to pole. There are 24 zones, each one 15 degrees wide. It takes one hour for the sun to move across each strip, so all locations within that time zone use the same time. The time zone to the east is one hour ahead, and the time zone to the west is one hour behind.

So by flying east to a new time zone, you will have moved into the future. Head west, and you travel back into the past. If you fly westward over the International Date Line—which runs through the Pacific Ocean—you will jump forward to the following day. Cross the line in the other direction, and you will end up in the previous day all over again.

WHERE IN THE WORLD?

We need time to navigate and find out where we are. Any location on Earth can be pinpointed using two numbers, the latitude and longitude. Latitude measures distance north or south of the equator. The equator has a latitude of 0°, while the North Pole is 90° north. Sailors figure out their latitude by measuring the altitude of the sun, or its angle above the horizon.

Longitude measures distance east or west. It is more difficult to measure. Lines of longitude run as great circles around Earth from pole to pole. They are all measured from the 0° line, which runs through Greenwich, London. To figure out the longitude, a sailor notes noon, when the sun reaches the highest point in the sky.

The line of 0° longitude at Greenwich is known as the Greenwich meridian.

BEHIND THE THEORY

Building a clock that was accurate at sea was an engineering challenge. The motion of a ship disturbed the clockwork, so clocks lost time on a voyage. The problem was solved by the British clockmaker John Harrison, who tried for 30 years to win a competition set by the Royal Navy for a clock that would be accurate at sea. Using high-quality materials and precision engineering, Harrison produced his marine **chronometer** in 1759. It was highly accurate—but it had cost more to create than the ship it sailed on!

The H4 was John Harrison's first successful chronometer.

The sailor then compares the difference between the local time and the time at Greenwich, as shown by the ship's chronometer, a tough clock. Every minute of difference accounts for a quarter of a degree; every hour means 15 degrees of difference. So if the local noon is two hours behind noon at Greenwich, the ship is 30 degrees west—out in the Atlantic Ocean. If it is 11 hours ahead of Greenwich, then the ship is sailing 165 degrees east in the Pacific Ocean. (Sailors also measure distance in nautical miles. Each nautical mile is equal to one minute of longitude—1.15 miles or 1,852 m. A speed of one knot equals one nautical mile an hour.)

CHAPTER 6

TIME CHALLENGES

Given that time may not really exist, people have learned a lot about it. However, are we still missing something? Is there a key that will unlock a new understanding of time—and time travel?

Einstein's theories of relativity have been shown to be true many times. Astronomers can see starlight bending as Einstein predicted as it shines past stars that warp space with their gravity. Experiments with clocks prove that time slows as Einstein predicted. However, in the century since Einstein had his ideas, other scientists have made many more discoveries that may lead us to building a time machine one day.

The light from distant **galaxies** like this is warped by the gravity of giant stars as it passes by.

In the 1920s, the English mathematician Paul Dirac figured out the mathematics for describing **electrons** and other small-matter particles. This was part of the basis for what is now called **quantum physics**.

Dirac's calculations also showed that it was possible for an **antimatter** version of an electron to exist. After some searching, the antimatter particle was discovered in 1932. It was named the positron because it resembles the electron in virtually every way, except that it has a positive charge while the electron has a negative one. The positron's behavior is like an electron's behavior running backward. It is as if a positron is traveling the other way through time.

Since the 1930s, scientists have discovered that there is almost no antimatter in the universe. When an antimatter particle meets its opposite matter particle, the pair **annihilate** each other into nothingness. One way of looking at these annihilations is that an electron is sent back in time and turned into a positron—the one that annihilated the electron! In quantum physics, time is every bit as weird as it is according to the theory of relativity. But another 1920s discovery revealed something almost as strange—every time we see a star, we are looking back in time.

Matter and antimatter particles destroy each other whenever they meet.

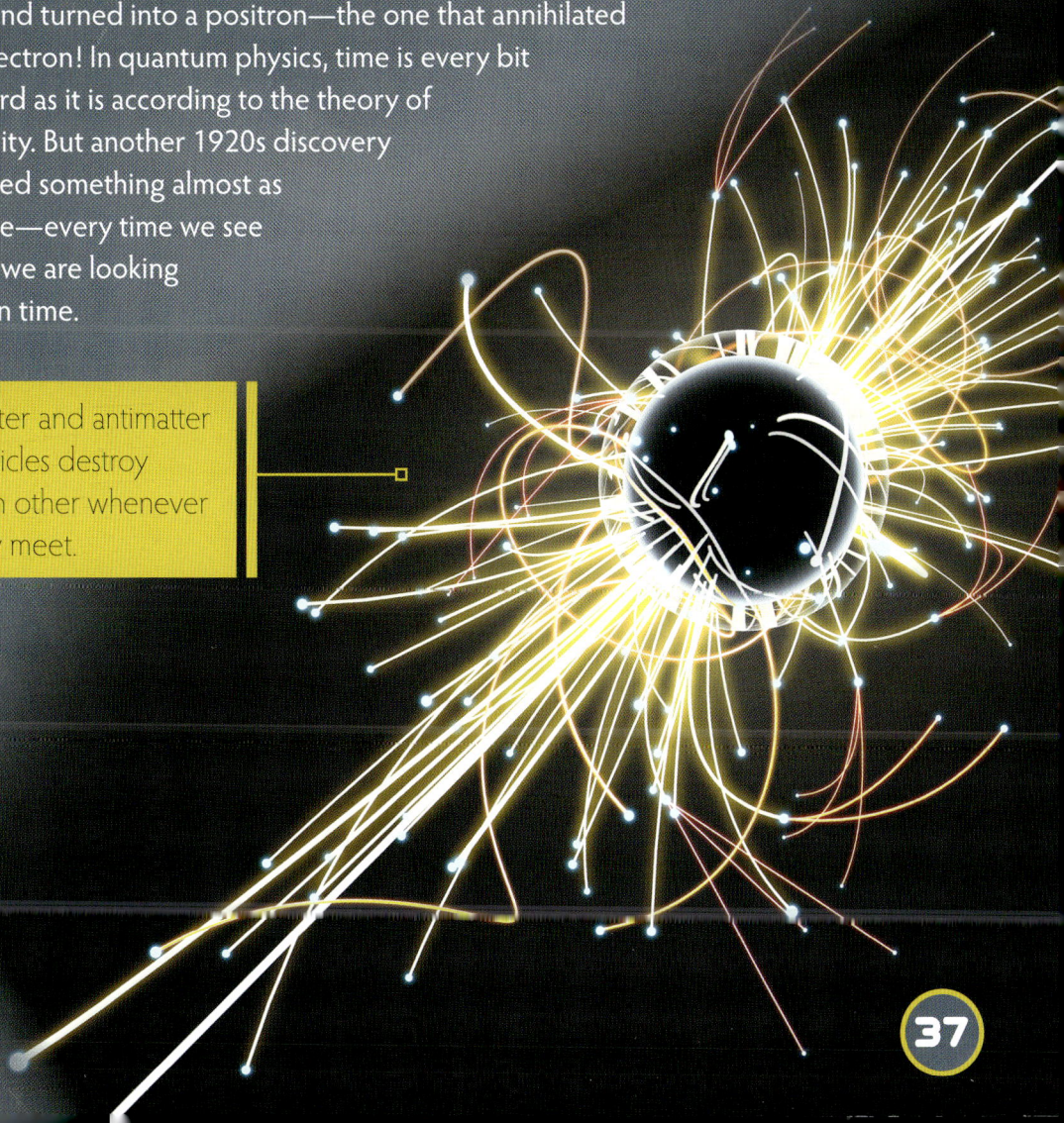

LOOKING FOR
THE BEGINNING

In 1929, the American astronomer Edwin Hubble discovered that the universe was expanding. Wherever we look in the sky, the stars and galaxies are zooming away from us. The universe has been expanding for a long time, so it is very large. It takes a long time for starlight to reach us across space. Distances in space are measured in **light-years**, or how far light travels in a year. The closest stars to us are in the Alpha Centauri system. They are four light-years away, meaning we see them as they appeared four years in the past. They might have exploded in the meantime, but we will not know on Earth until light from the explosion reaches us.

The closest stars to Earth are Alpha Centauri and Proxima Centauri, the two bright lights in this photograph.

UNANSWERED

Astronomers describe the first few thousand years of time as the Dark Ages. That might seem like an odd name, because at the time the universe was very hot, which would also suggest that it would have been very bright. However, energy and matter were squeezed together so tightly that there was no room for light to shine through. Because no light will ever reach us from that time, it is invisible to telescopes. The earliest days of the universe will stay hidden from view.

Around 1,000 years ago, astronomers in Arabia and China recorded seeing a new star in the sky. The bright object faded to become what is called the Crab Nebula. People had previously believed the heavens were unchanging. The new star was evidence that the universe changed in time, as new stars appeared and old ones faded away. The Crab Nebula was produced by an exploding giant star. What we see of it today formed when humans were still inventing agriculture and building the first cities.

The rate at which the universe is expanding suggests that it is about 13.8 billion years old. Looking at galaxies more than 13 billion light-years away from Earth is like looking back to the dawn of time. Astronomers' telescopes work like time machines.

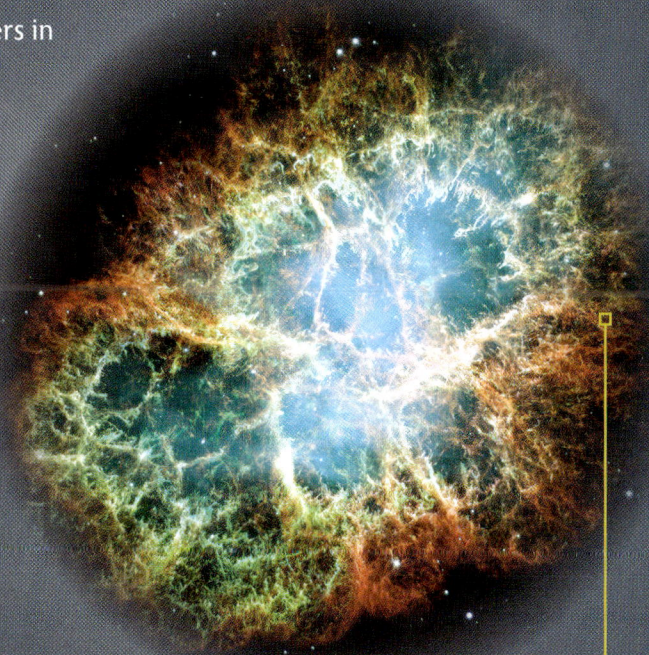

We see the Crab Nebula today as it was 7,000 years ago.

WHAT CAUSES NOW?

Another way of describing the speed of light is as the speed of causality—the rate at which change spreads through the universe. Our understanding of time requires that every effect has a cause, which must be further back in time than the effect. A cause from one place must travel in space to produce an effect somewhere else—and it cannot move faster than light, because nothing moves faster than light.

At the quantum scale, however, cause and effect get weird. Quantum physics includes a phenomenon called entanglement, where the properties of subatomic particles are closely linked. If you change one particle, the other alters to mirror it. **Lasers** create entangled light particles called **photons**, which stay entangled even after they move off in opposite directions.

A long, narrow laser beam is created from electromagnetic **radiation**.

What no one can explain is that entanglement creates an instantaneous link between the particles. A change in one creates an immediate change in another—even if they are billions of light-years apart. That means cause and effect are happening faster than light, which is against the rules of time.

Does that mean our theories about energy, space, and time are wrong? Not really. In quantum physics nothing is true until you measure it. Before that, scientists can only know the chances of something being true.

UNANSWERED

To illustrate the complexities of quantum physics, imagine two scientists measuring entangled particles. The first scientist measures their particle and gets a value of 1. That means the other particle must have a value of 0, as they are matter and antimatter. That information can travel at no faster than the speed of light to their partner, who learns that their particle has a measurement of 0. If the second scientist makes their measurement before receiving the information, they have a 50 percent chance of getting either 1 or 0 as a result. They get 0 but have no way of knowing whether this result was an effect—or a cause.

COULD WE BUILD A TIME MACHINE?

Science describes the universe in two main ways. Relativity covers the big picture, while quantum physics covers the tiniest particles. Neither of them describe time anything like we experience it in everyday life. One reason for this may be that the universe has more dimensions than the four we use. That would mean the universe is filled with hyperspace, or space outside of our space. The universe might also contain hypertime, a time filled with alternative histories.

The best chance of being able to travel in time is a wormhole. A wormhole is a path, or tube, through hyperspace. It starts at one place in space and ends at a point far away. The wormhole's hyperspace path may be shorter than the distance between the two mouths through space.

Wormholes are known as Einstein–Rosen bridges for Albert Einstein and Nathan Rosen, who showed in 1935 that they could exist—in theory.

Using a wormhole
to teleport to
another time is
an attractive idea—
but highly unlikely.

In that case, the mouths could
also connect different points
in time. A time machine could
use a wormhole to connect with
a time of our choosing.

No natural wormhole has ever been
found. An artificial wormhole might be
made by warping space so that distant points
are folded next to each other, then using negatve energy to push space
apart. Once time travelers entered a wormhole, however, they would not
be able to return to tell us their experiences—unless they created another
wormhole to come back to the present. So it looks as if humans are destined
not to learn about the future of time and time travel until we get there—but
only time will tell!

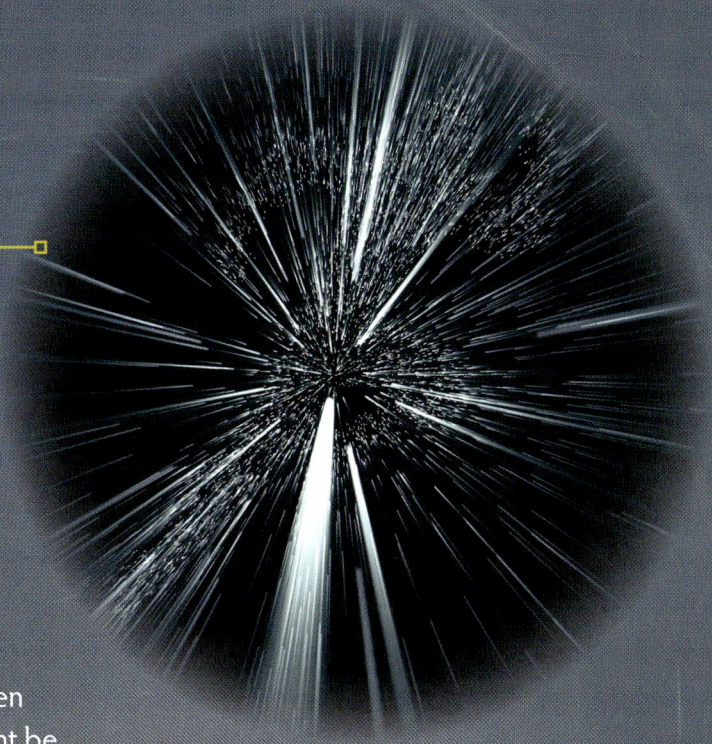

UNANSWERED

The far end of a wormhole would be a white hole. This
is the opposite of a black hole. A black hole has such
huge gravity that nothing can escape, even light. A white
hole expels everything—including the time traveler. Like
wormholes, white holes are an idea that comes out of
the mathematics used to understand relativity. However,
while we have good evidence of black holes forming from
collapsing stars, white holes break many laws of physics.

TIMELINE

C.4000 BC The Chinese use water clocks to measure the passage of time.

C.1600 BC The monument at Stonehenge is completed in its modern shape. It is possibly moved to measure the passage of the sun during the year.

C.1500 BC The Egyptians begin using sundials to measure time.

1270s Thomas Aquinas proposes that God is the prime mover who set time and the universe in motion.

1410 A mechanical clock is built in Prague to track the movement of astronomical bodies.

1602 Galileo Galilei observes that a pendulum moves at a constant speed.

1687 Isaac Newton publishes his laws of motion, which describe a universe of interrelated causes and effects.

1759 John Harrison invents the first successful marine chronometer, H4.

1814 Pierre-Simon Laplace describes a situation in which knowing the future of the universe would mean that that future was already determined.

1855 Rudolf Clausius proposes the law of entropy, which states that energy is dissipated.

1866 James Clerk Maxwell proposes that nothing can travel faster than the speed of light.

1884	The idea of Universal Coordinated Time (UTC) is first adopted.
1916	Albert Einstein describes the workings of a "relativistic" universe in the General Theory of Relativity.
1927	George Lemaitre proposes a theory of the creation of the universe now known as the Big Bang Theory.
1929	U.S. astronomer Edwin Hubble observes that the universe is constantly expanding.
1930	English mathematician Paul Dirac publishes the book *On the Principles of Quantum Mechanics*, summing up his studies of subatomic particles.
1932	The existence of the antimatter positron is confirmed.
1935	Albert Einstein and Nathan Rosen propose the existence of wormholes in space; the phenomena are also known as Einstein–Rosen bridges.
1975	The term "chaos theory" is coined to describe a situation in which a small variation in the input to a system can have massive consequences on its output.
1980s	String theory emerges as an alternate way to explain the behavior of energy and time.
2016	NASA studies the effects of space travel on the astronaut Scott Kelly by comparing him to his twin, Mark, who remained on Earth.

GLOSSARY

annihilate to cause something to cease to exist

antimatter particles that are the antiparticles that make up normal matter

astronomers people who study space

atomic clocks clocks that use the movement of electrons

atoms the smallest particles that can exist

causality the principle that something causes something else to happen or exist

chronometer a highly accurate clock

dimensions measurable extents of qualities such as height or mass

electrons subatomic particles in the nuclei of atoms

entropy the degree of disorder in a system

free will the ability to decide one's own actions

friction the resistance between two moving surfaces

galaxies systems of millions or billions of stars held together by gravity

gravity the force by which all physical bodies attract one another

heavy metals dense metals of high atomic weight

infinite having no ending or beginning

instantaneous happening at the same time

lasers devices that generate intense beams of concentrated light

light-years units of distance based on how far light travels in one year, 5.9 trillion miles (9.5 trillion km)

mass the quantity of matter something contains

matter the substance of which physical objects are made

observatory a building that houses a telescope

orbit to follow a regular path around a star or other body in space

oscillations regular back-and-forth movements

paradox a seemingly absurd suggestion that is possibly true

particles tiny pieces of matter

philosophers people who think about serious questions of existence

photons particles of energy

physics the science of matter and energy

practical able to be put into practice

predetermined already decided

quantum related to the smallest possible quantities of matter and energy

quantum physics the branch of science that explains the behavior of atoms and subatomic particles

quartz a hard mineral

radiation a stream of energy

relativity how phenomena are related to one another

warping a bending out of shape

FOR MORE INFORMATION

BOOKS

Keranen, Rachel. *The Big Bang Theory.* New York, NY: Cavendish Square Publishing, 2017.

Latta, Sara. *Black Holes: The Weird Science of the Most Mysterious Objects in the Universe.* Minneapolis, MN: Twenty-First Century Books, 2017.

May, Brian. *Exploring the Mysteries of the Universe.* New York, NY: Rosen Young Adult, 2016.

Nardo, Don. *Hubble Deep Field: How a Photo Revolutionized Our Understanding of the Universe.* North Mankato, MN: Compass Point Books, 2017.

Roland, James. *Black Holes: A Space Discovery Guide.* Minneapolis, MN: Lerner Publications, 2017.

WEBSITES

www.dkfindout.com/uk/space/stars-and-galaxies/big-bang
A Dorling Kindersley page about the creation of the universe in the Big Bang.

https://starchild.gsfc.nasa.gov/docs/StarChild/universe_level2/cosmology.html
A guide to cosmology from the Star Child project at NASA.

www.ducksters.com/science/physics/theory_of_relativity.php
A Ducksters page about the theory of relativity, which is the basis of our current understanding of the universe.

www.esa.int/esaKIDSen/SEM0V1BE8JG_OurUniverse_0.html
European Space Agency pages about the structure of the universe.

Publisher's note to educators and parents: Our editors have carefully reviewed these websites to ensure that they are suitable for students. Many websites change frequently, however, and we cannot guarantee that a site's future contents will continue to meet our high standards of quality and educational value. Be advised that students should be closely supervised whenever they access the Internet.

INDEX